SUCH MEAN ESTATE

SUCH MEAN ESTATE

RYAN SPENCER

Essay by LESLIE JAMISON

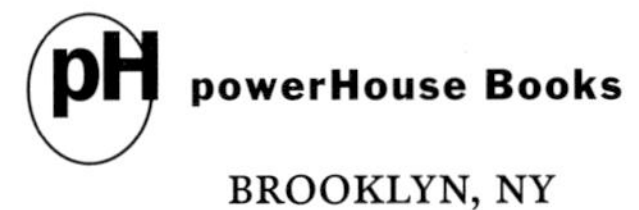

powerHouse Books

BROOKLYN, NY

For my nephew Christopher, one of our young inheritors.
The world is yours to burn or not.

Catechism
LESLIE JAMISON

What does the sky hold?
Too many birds. Broken freeways. The frail limbs of a charred forest. Blindness if you stare straight at the sun. Helicopters swarming the sky like mosquitoes, then smoked propellers falling past the sign reading BUY LARGE. We did.

Where does danger live?
In the salt swell and the spider's web; in the burnt trees and the child at the door and the parking lot where the undead hordes are wandering. A woman in suburbia has blood on her shoulder. Something explodes in the distance. Look closer: also blood on her hands. She killed for breakfast. She smeared the dead thing on her toast.

Where does the light come from?
From comets and bombs; from the blistering sun. From flash-lights trained across a dark swamp in the dead of night. Bright-ness begins as something circled by birds; becomes the gleam

reflected in the goggles of a scientist. It keeps bleeding into dawn over a doomed city. It sharpens into a pair of headlights just before a man steps out of the truck to shoot up the fog. Light becomes the still point once more. Birds wheel around it. It catches glints of a broken freeway. It ghosts the big clouds. It haunts the aftermath.

Is the light hope?
Sometimes we row our little boats toward it. We keep our fingers crossed.

But?
Sometimes it explodes. Sometimes it's a living terror in the sky. Sometimes hope is a little girl holding her own severed arm in the street. Sometimes a boy raises his fist to the exploding sky. Whenever a man and a woman stare at an explosion, a part of them is already fucking under it. They are glistening with someone's sweat, or someone's blood, or some sky's rain; and somewhere deep inside their tired bodies they are getting ready to help the human race survive.

Did we do this to ourselves?
We make traffic jams trying to escape the world we've built. We bought too large. We exhaled too long. The boy on the trampoline jumps so high that his head disappears from the frame. Now he lives without his eyes. Dad watches the sky split open like it was his favorite sitcom playing syndicated. The woman with golden earrings glances over her shoulder to catch sight of the horizon catching fire. Clouds roasted like marshmallows; everything—eventually—scorched beyond simile. A man stands behind a flag so his eyes are gone too. Or gone to us. He sees only stripes. Another man stands at the edge of an overpass, deciding whether he should jump. Whenever someone looks beyond the frame, you wonder what they're looking for—some kind of answer; some kind of monster.

When the voice cries out in the middle of the night, whose voice is it?
The girl in the doorway. The boy in the doorway. The man who believes he is about to die. The man who believes he is the only one who hasn't died already. The man dangling at the lip of a distant cave, holding on. His whisper carries.

Where is refuge?
It's Prince Street strung with sparkly stars. It's the possibility of Zac Hobson still alive. It's the hushed tones of a child asking: What do we do now? It's the Cedar Creek Elementary School, where everyone is directed for the duration of the quarantine. Men with guns show them the way.

Who will live and who will die?
Everyone will die.

Yes. But who now?
The old man with goggles, who goes poking at the spider. The woman drinking swamp-water like moonshine. Three people drag a fourth from the waves. High tide brings new corpses; low tide shows the ones already there.

What about the man on the overpass?
Maybe he decides to go. Maybe he decides to stay.

And we give up on knowing?
I'm only saying we don't know about the figure at the doorway. She's coming to kill you or else she's coming to save you. It's hard to say for sure. The light behind her is blinding. Living in the dark place makes you believe in anything. A woman in a tailored suit—with a pearl bracelet—shuts the shop door neatly behind her. Never trust the ones who are dressed well when the world ends. They've got plans. They're looking out

for themselves. Two men in white suits hold the prone body of a woman between them. Maybe they've knocked her out; maybe they're trying to save her life. Maybe she was the woman at the doorway. She's at another doorway now. The end of the world dissolves the story and leaves us with still frames. We piece them together the best we can.

What do people watch from doorways?
The pieces. The piecing together. A single pony standing on a concrete terrace while the sea keeps rustling behind him. The body of a watching boy is holy.

And other bodies?
Other bodies are turning into the mist; or touching each other quietly, cradled by dawn. The child's body is sharply outlined at the doorway. She is waiting for the killer, or the tsunami, or her period. And his body—the boy's—is bent by light; as if

curdled, milk turned from age or sun. His arm crooked back as if shielding from whatever can't be kept at bay for long. Bodies are looking for other bodies in the night. Bodies are out of proportion, out of luck, out of time, out of frame. That boy on his trampoline. He's just trying to jump high enough to ditch the movie he got stuck inside of.

Why can't we see any faces?
When we're watching the end of the world, we're all facing the same direction. We see the backs of heads. We see curly hair singed and sifting soot like dandruff. One woman stares at the ocean and her hair is like snakes, or like a sculpture of snakes. We brush and brush and brush and the wind turns everything to tangles. We see faces with explosions behind them—the explosions dim everything else black. Features get rubbed away into darkness. A man with a bald spot watches the world collapse into rubble. Time has taken his hair, his

youth, and now this—everything else. It gets hot in his sweater. A wool cardigan makes you sweat when the whole world is on fire. There is so much we can't know. We see each moment but we can't see the next one. Every story is obscured by fog or fire. Every story ends the same anyway: living bodies discover dead ones.

Tell me a story anyway.
A dark building is full of bright women, their pale skin blurred and glowing. They have been saved. They can remember days before they needed saving: staring at infinite oceans, curls swirling in the wind. They think of their unsaved husbands, protecting their unsaved children from rabid birds or stepping from their trucks to scan the fog for their wives. But these women aren't in that fog. They're behind these dark walls instead—horribly safe, beyond consolation.

Tell me another one.
A dark building is full of bright women, their pale skin blurred and glowing. They have been saved. They are for sale. They serve the men who survived. They dull the grief with their bodies: the ghosts of wives and sons. They stand in a line with their hands on each other's backs. They march slowly—once a week—to the wall at the edge of their world, where they set fire to the garbage they have brought. Sometimes the only warmth for miles is your own life burning.

Where are the birds going?
Over the city. Over the suburbs. Back to that still point of light. Their beaks bear gleaming bits of blood. Motion makes us wonder what happens past our range of vision. We keep watching because we want to know the world can be worse than what it already is; we want to scare ourselves and soothe ourselves at once—it can be that bad; it's not that bad yet.

The everyday goes strange and wondrous with devastation—
asphalt ripped up and rivers of lava running down our morning
commutes. All the women must be sweating in their hijabs.
Once the world ends, do they have permission to go without?

Are we the only people left?
Maybe there are people under the streets. Maybe there are scien-
tists left in the lab, secretly saving us. Maybe Zac Hobson, who
wrote his name on the billboard. But we must live as if we're all
there is.

How do we pray for the world?
It's too late for that.

Then what do we pray for?
We pray for the beginning of every ending: toilet water flushing
counterclockwise in the northern hemisphere, too much light-
ning or not enough wind, tsunamis littering beaches with the
old plastic of dead jellyfish, birds flying rabid into European
plazas, wolves dying of inexplicable disease above the perma-
frost. We thank god for the wolves and for their dying, because
how else would our lowly lupine expert become the only man
who can possibly save the world? We pray for the unlikely
heroes: the humble analyzer of DNA, the quiet arborist, the
loneliest ornithologist, the crypto-meteorologist in bifocals—
we need to see each man close his laptop and take a bullet or
an asteroid to the chest. We pray: Let him turn away from his
swivel chair, throw off his lab coat, clutch his sheath of charts
and surge forth into the gloaming. Let him sound the alarm.
Let him rise into his mythos. Let him claim the junior high
school that will someday bear his name.

Why do heroes need our prayers?
So they can become men again. So they can save their estranged
wives and disabled children from milky swamps or massive
spider webs, from tombs of snow tucked into the ruins of

skyscrapers. Let the peril of innocents drive our heroes onto snowplows, or speedboats, so they can ride over the frosted or flooded Eastern Seaboard while their sidekicks seduce the beautiful daughters of third-world presidents. Thank god for these fools' errands. We would feel nothing without them.

What else are we grateful for?
For keyboards that glow in the dark, for computers with their crawl spaces like circuit-studded stomachs, for men who run their flashlights over hushed and creaturely waters.

Where are the heroes hiding?
Past the concrete walls. Past the salt tides. They are saving themselves for the warehouse, the parking lot, the empty streets where the bodies are thickest.

What kind of ending do we request?
Let the cities of the world fall like dominoes: give us the leaning tower finally crashing into Pisa; give us Big Ben exploded and Cairo on fire; give us Tokyo businessmen fighting dolphins in the street. Give Manhattan to heaven and Los Angeles to hell. Give our meteorologist and his marriage a second chance in all the wreckage; give him a love that holds jellyfish strewn upon the sand like scarves. Let him shield his face from those armies of brown birds flying straight from the white hot eye of the sun. Let his sidekick fuck that dictator's girl at least once before the second meteor hits.

But please—in the end, at the last—let the second meteor hit. Don't deny anyone his junior high school. Let everyone fall into the asteroid chasm. Let everyone blister in the too-close sun. Let everyone perish. Let no one live.

Why do we like to watch ourselves die?
Because we step outside, into the light, and get to live again.

What do we do now?
One step, and then another.
Buy small. Breathe in flame. Breathe out song.

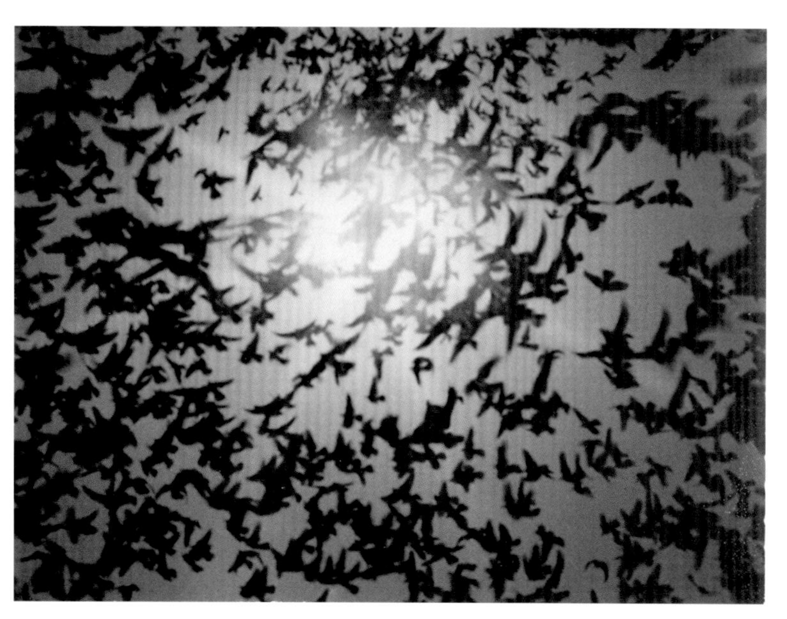

Why lies He in such mean estate
Where ox and ass are feeding?
Good Christian, fear: for sinners here
The silent Word is pleading.

—WILLIAM CHATTERTON DIX
"What Child Is This?"
1865

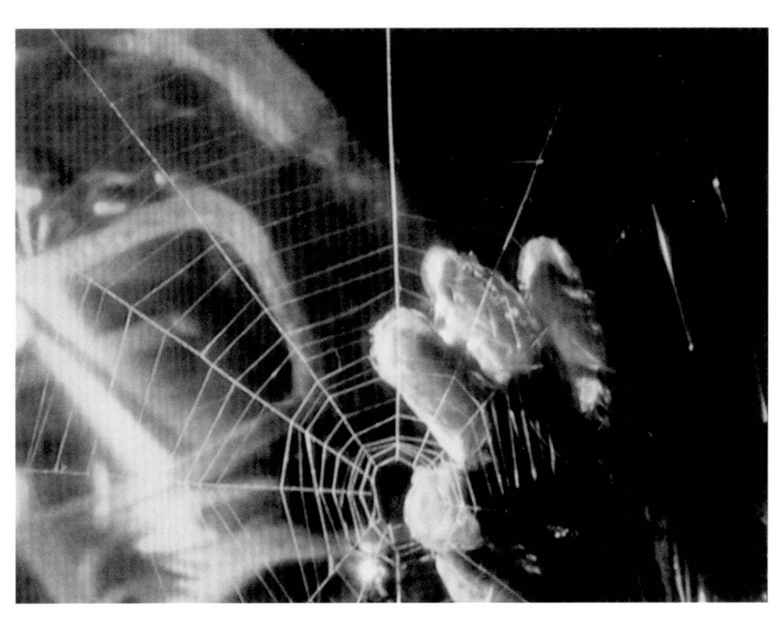

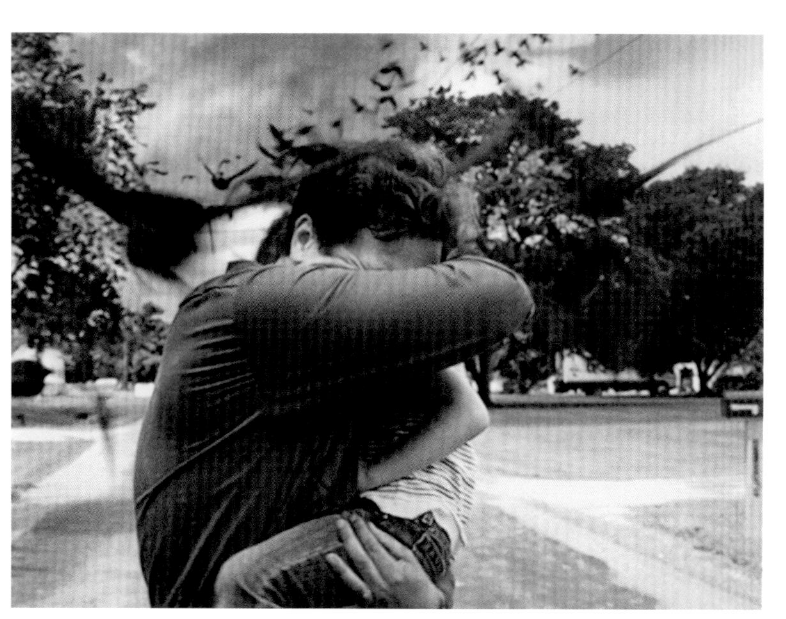

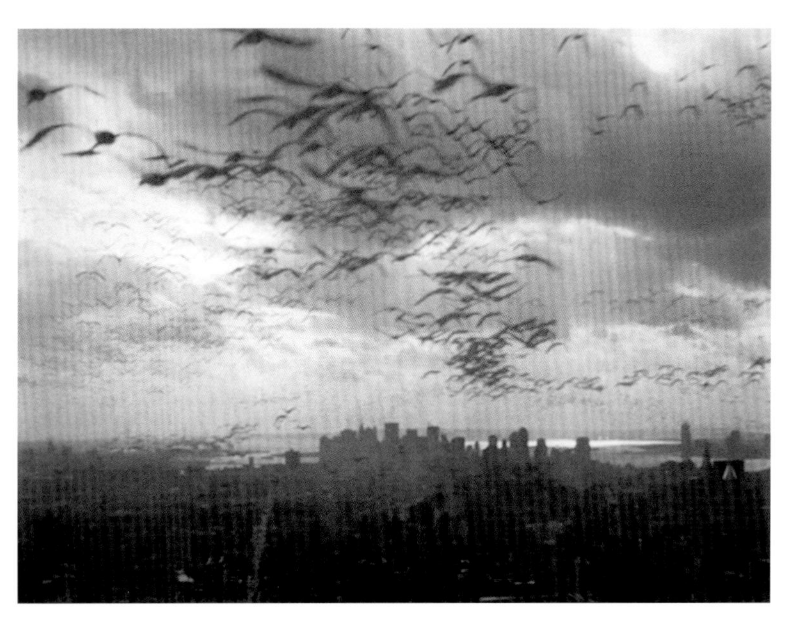

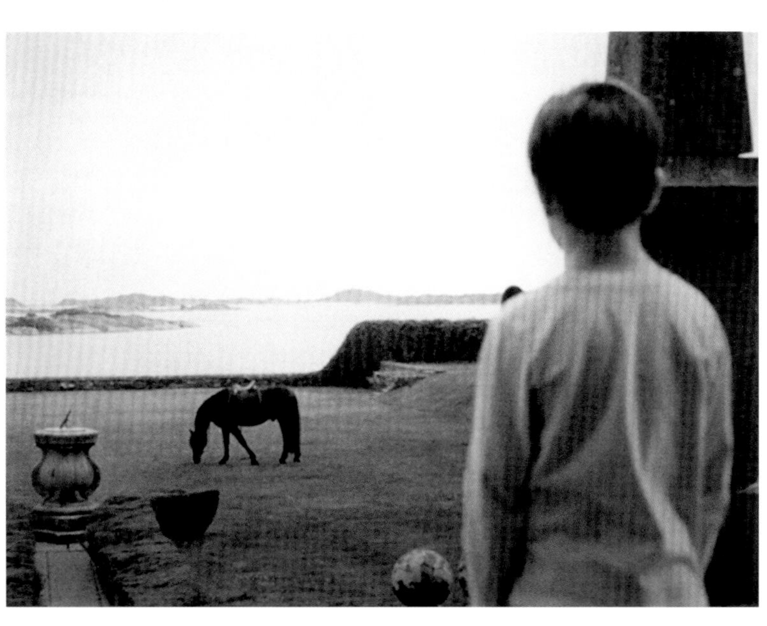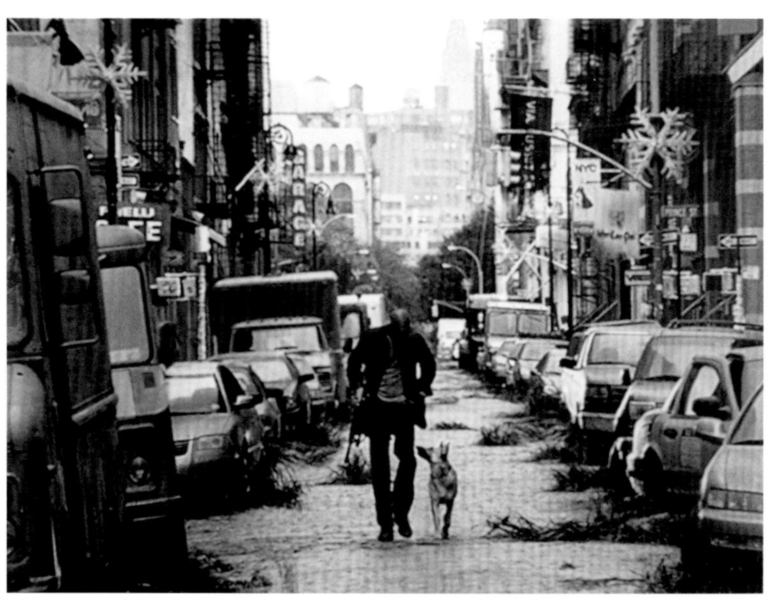

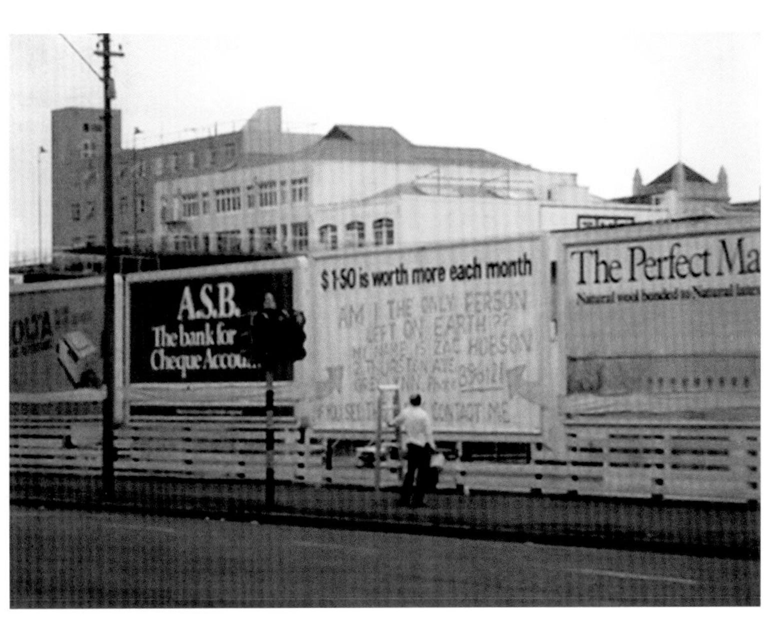
$1·50 is worth more each month
A.S.B.
The bank for
Cheque Accounts
The Perfect Ma
Natural wool bonded to Natural latex

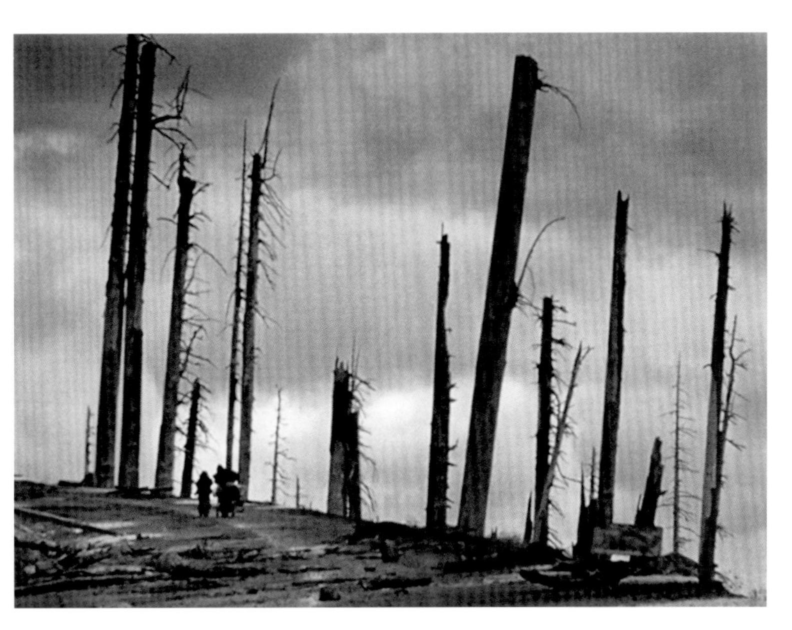

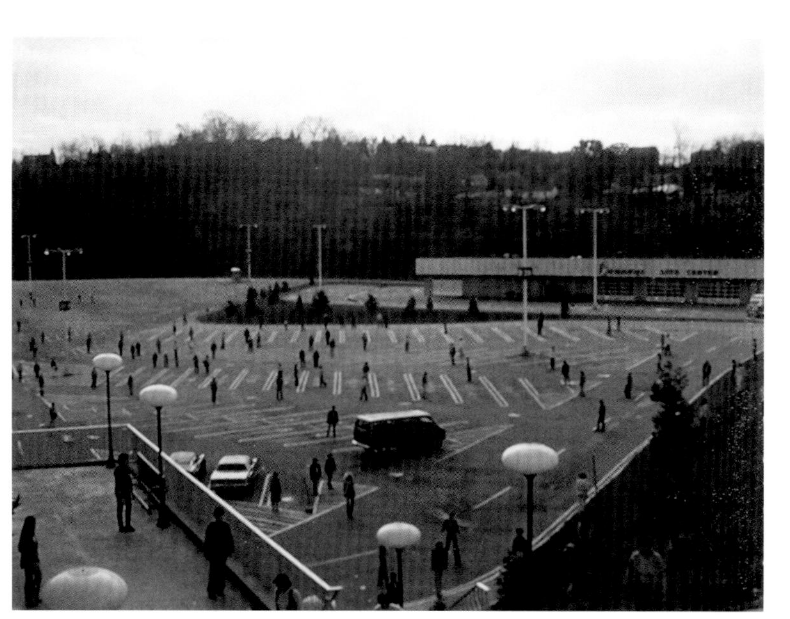

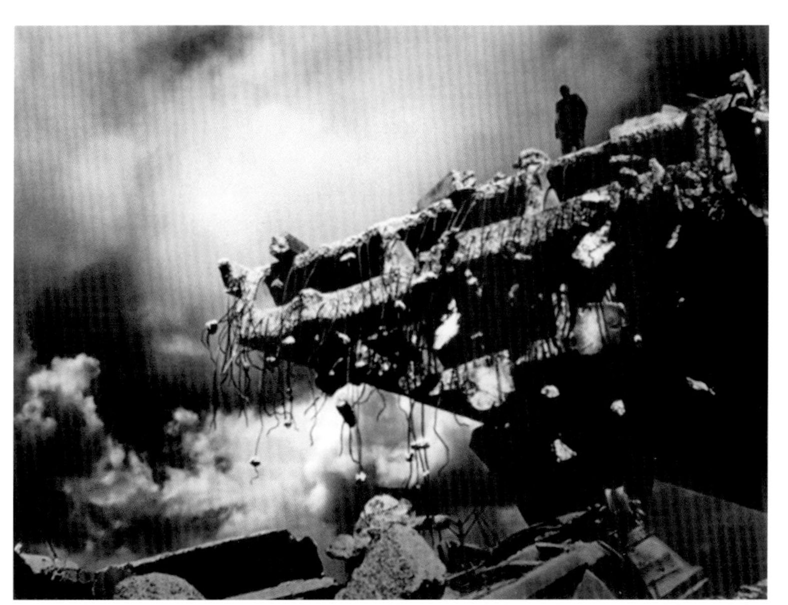

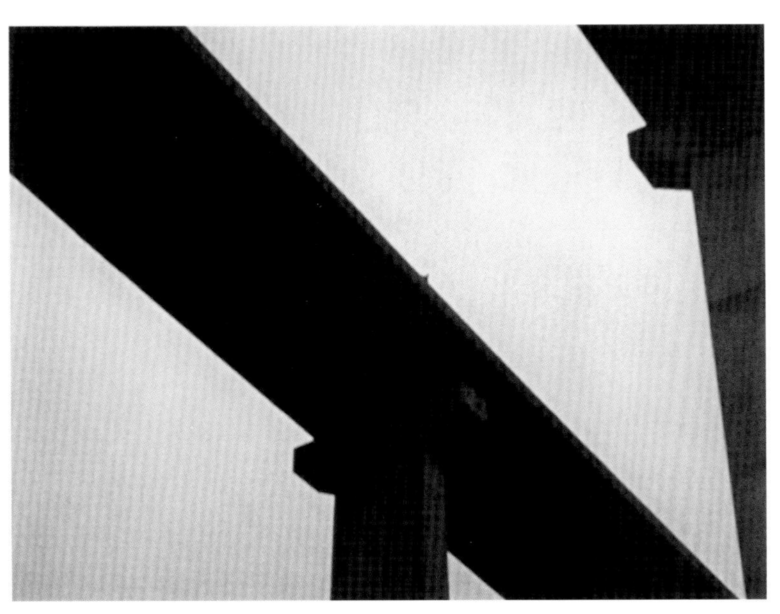

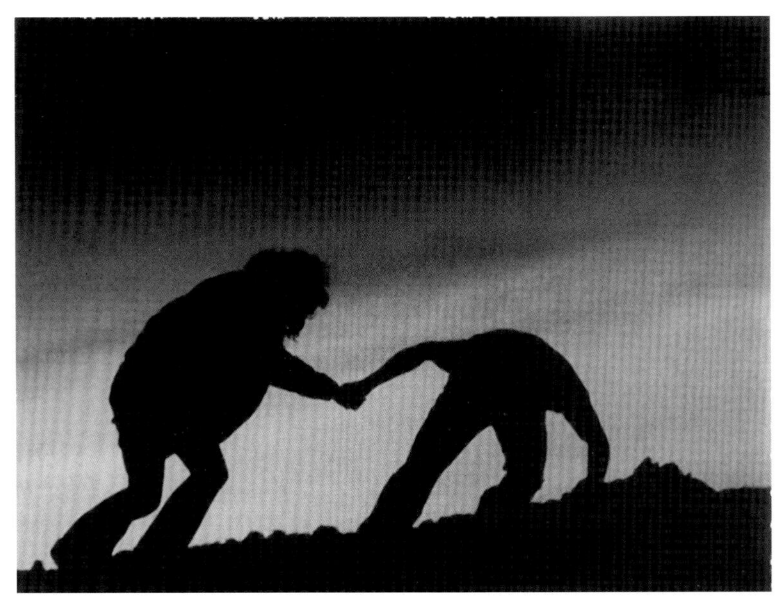

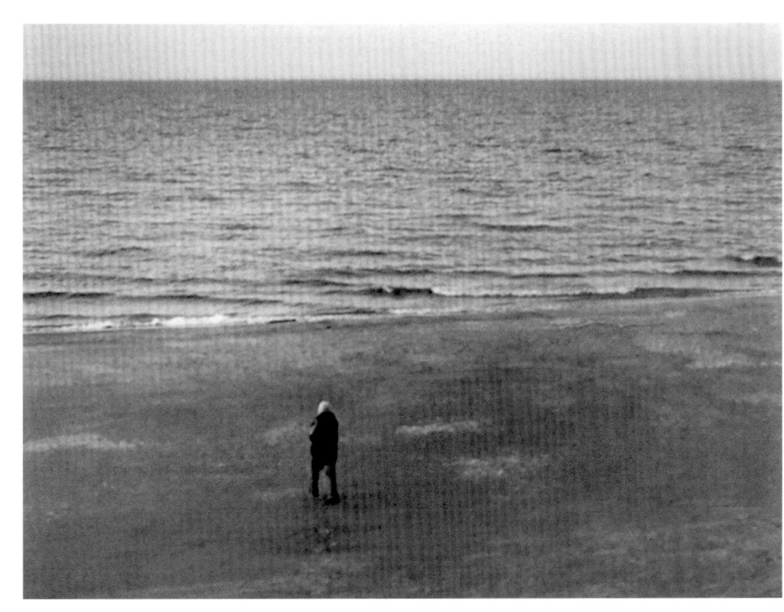

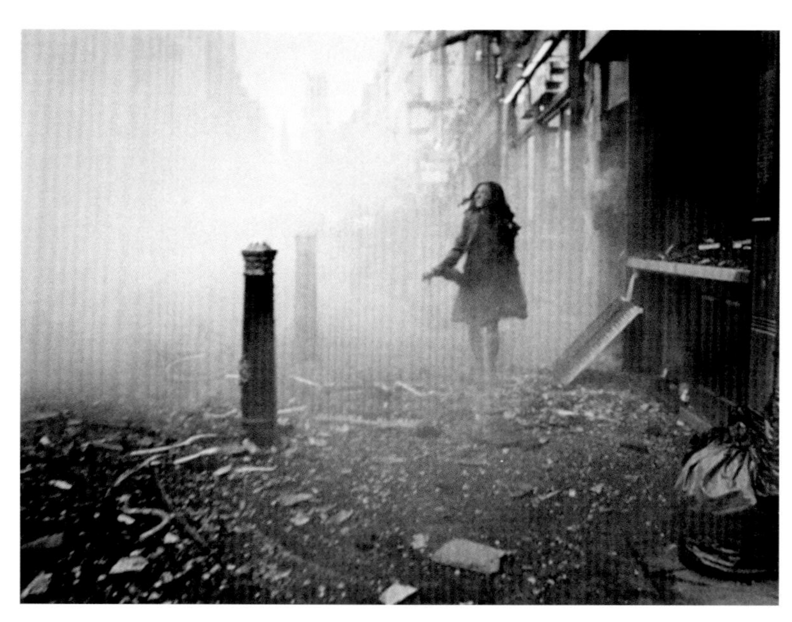

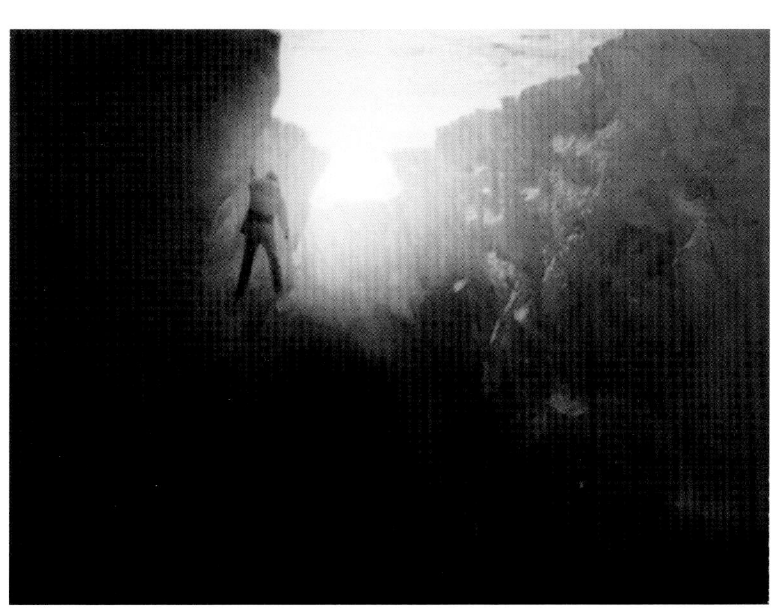

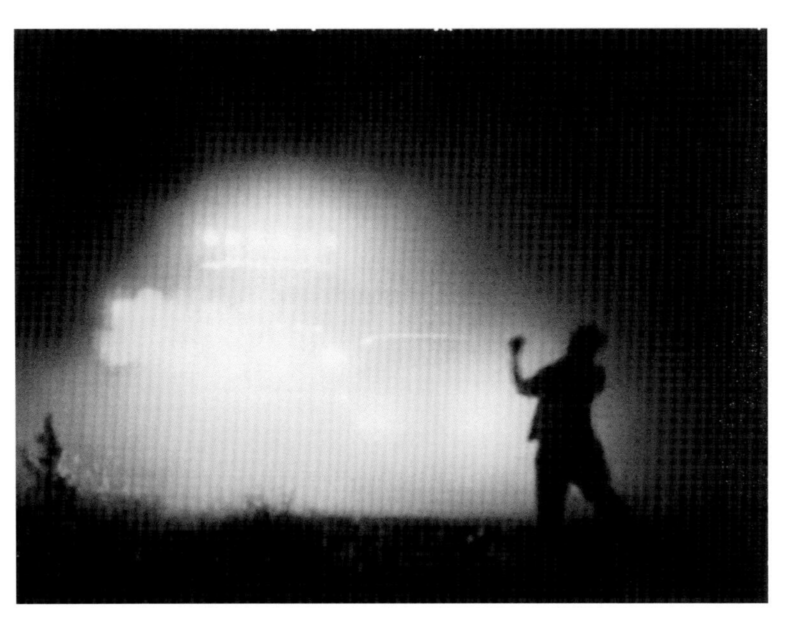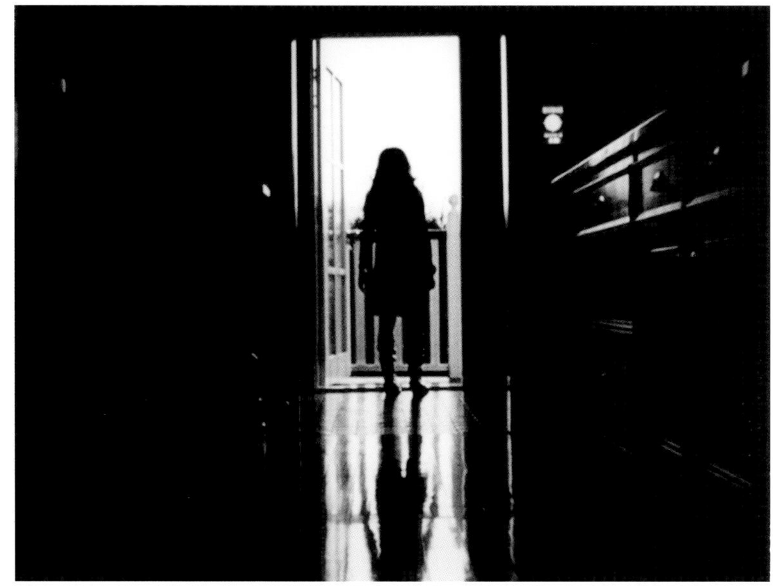

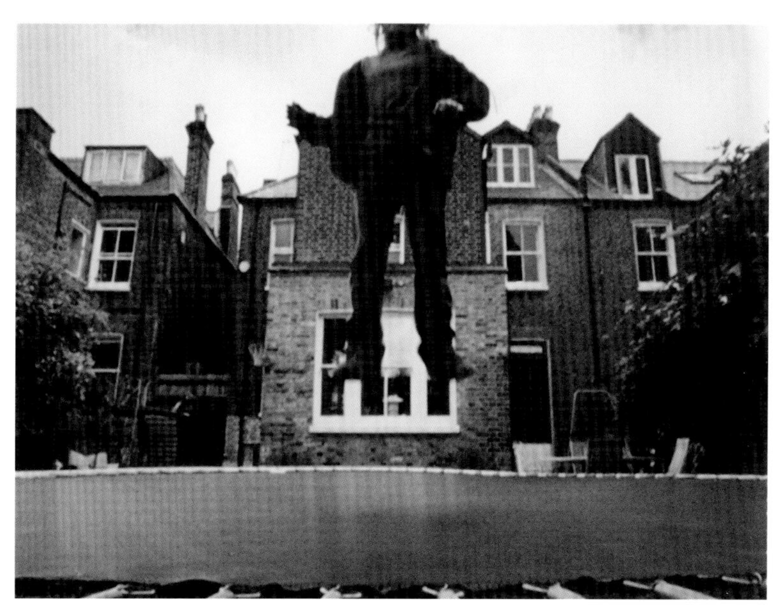

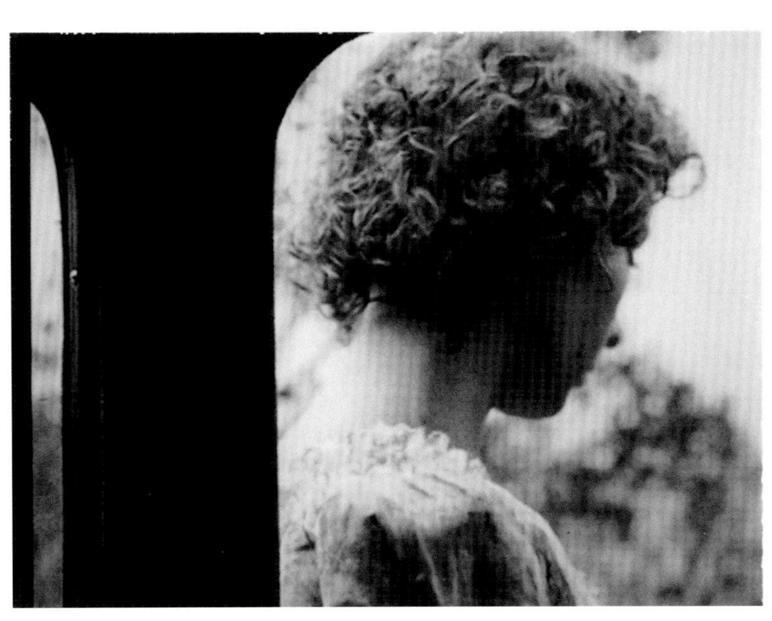 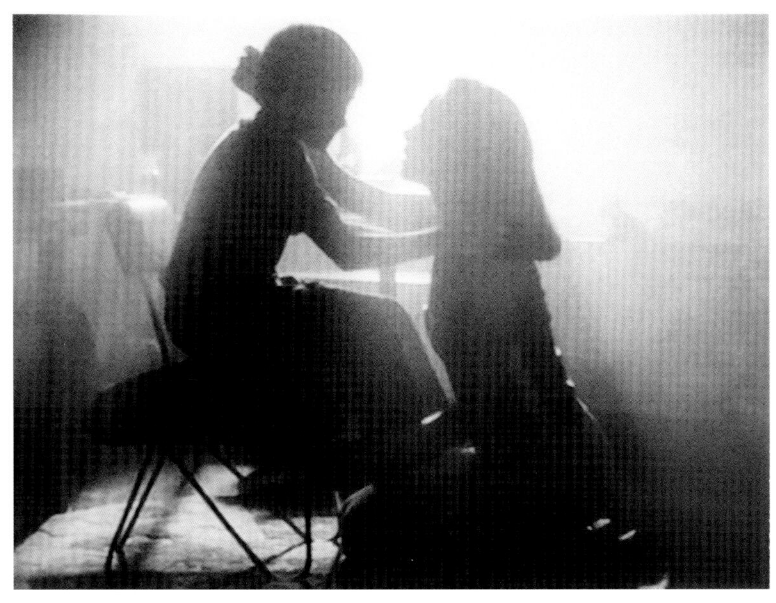

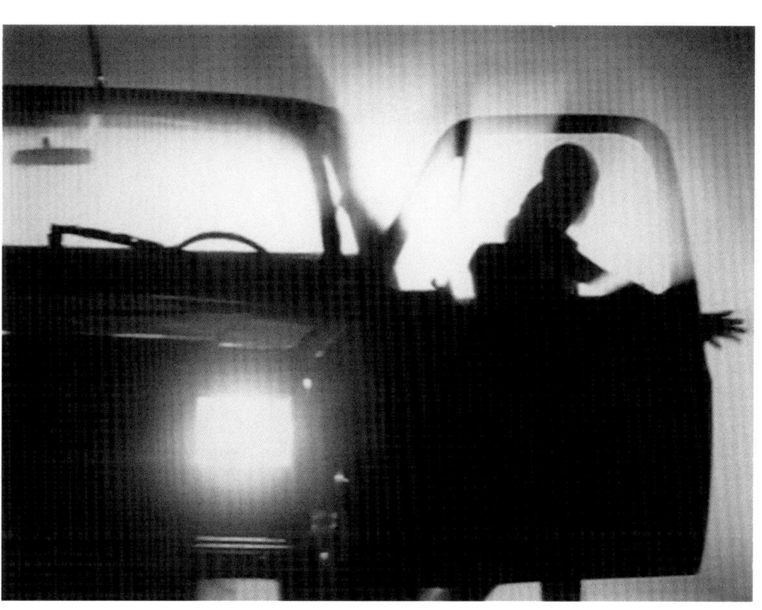

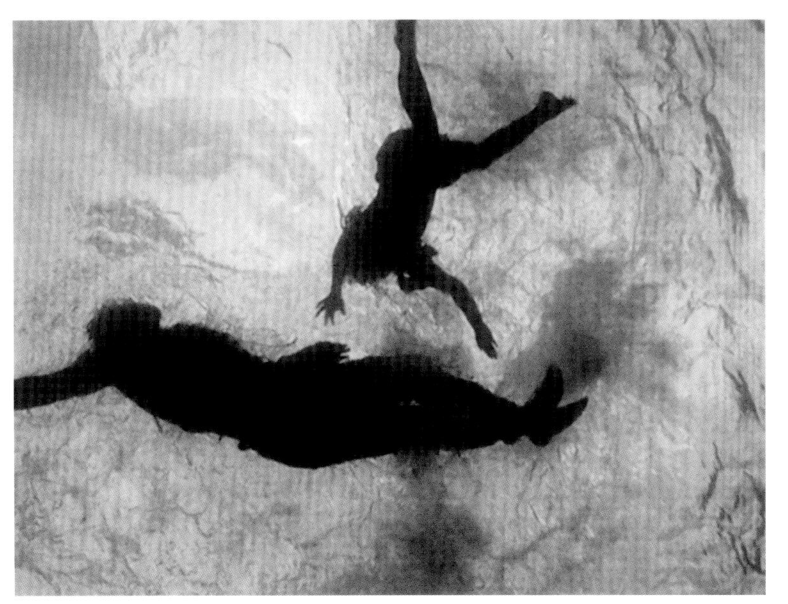

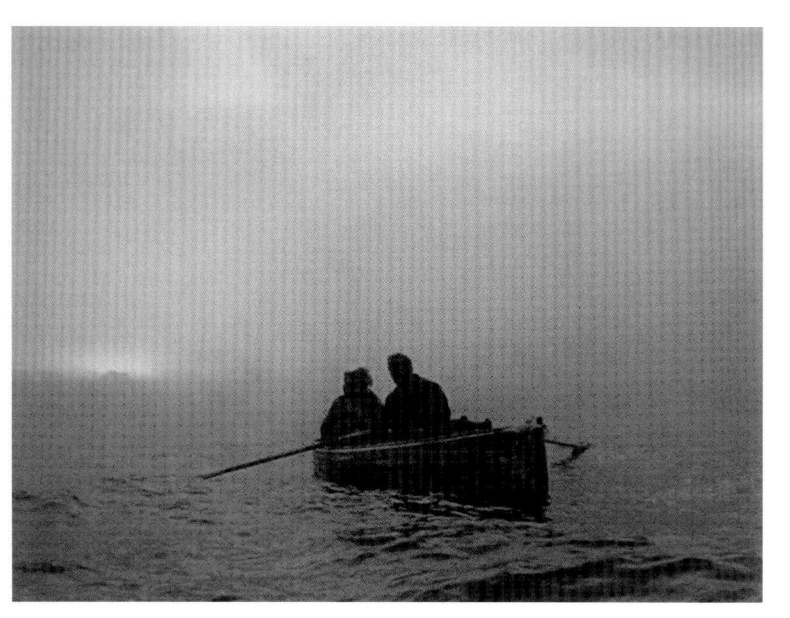

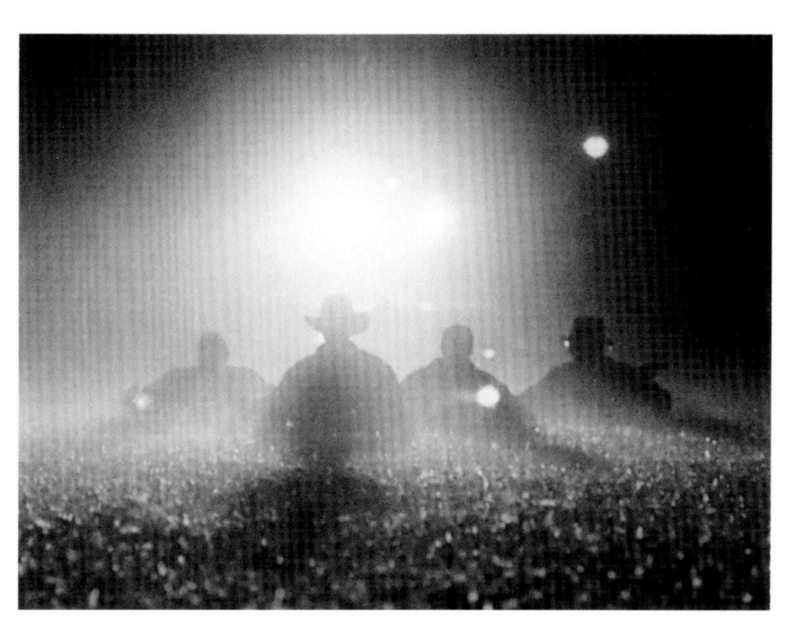

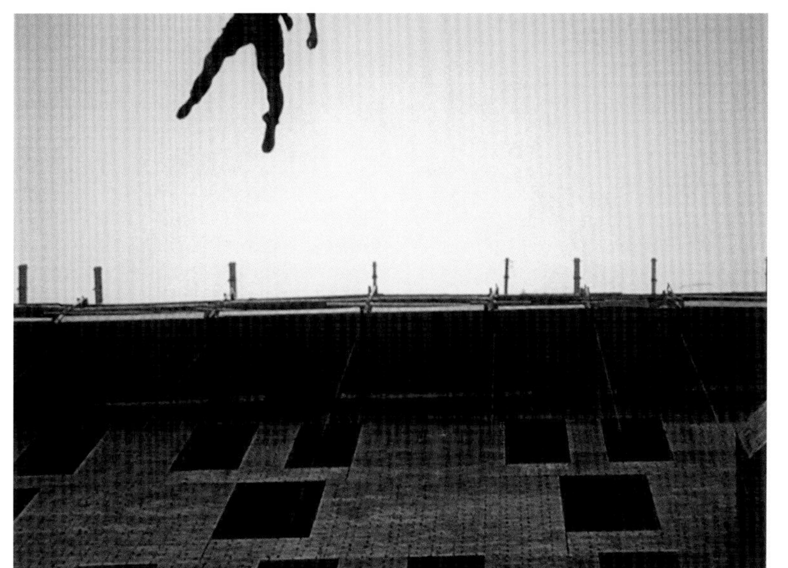

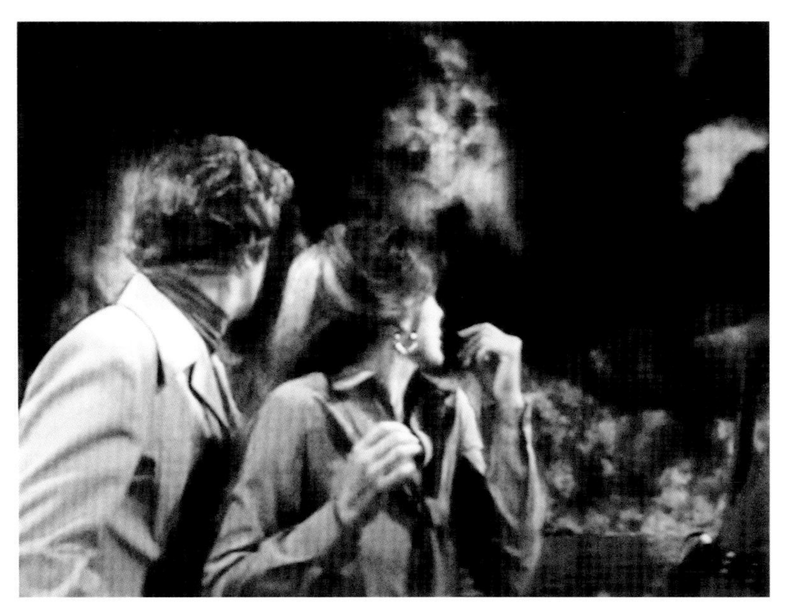

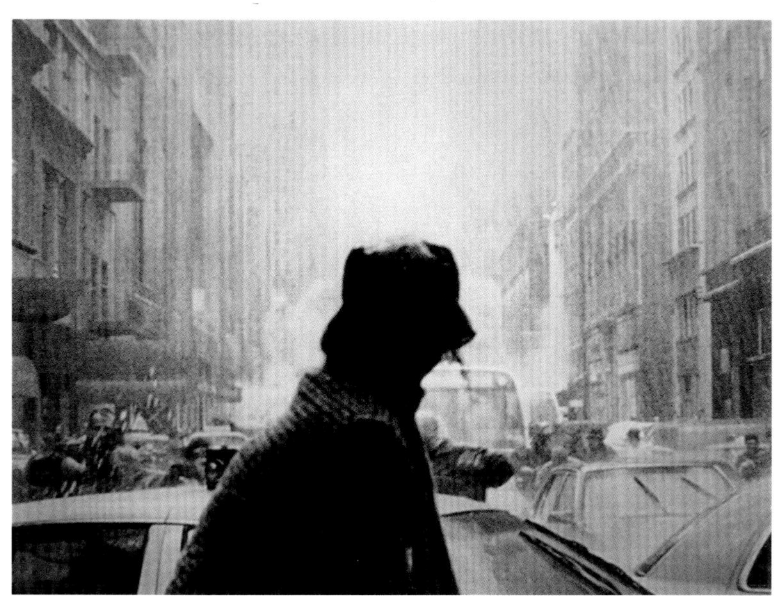

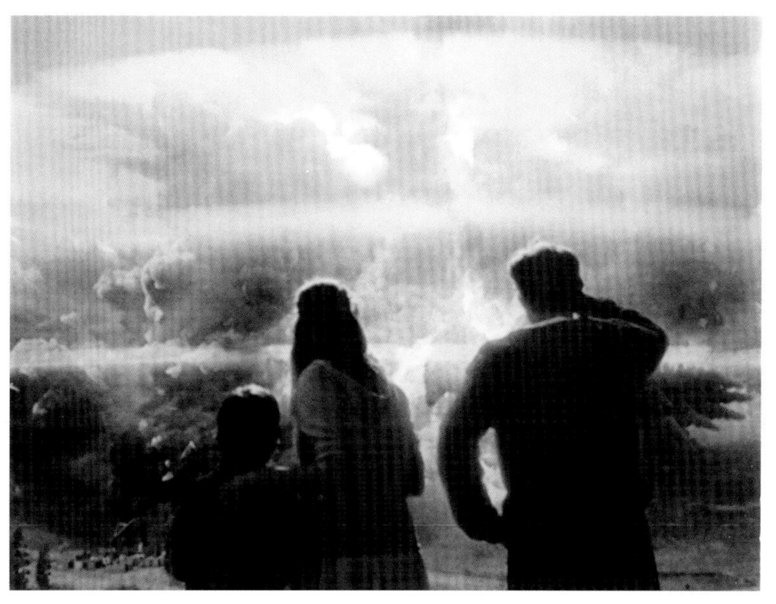

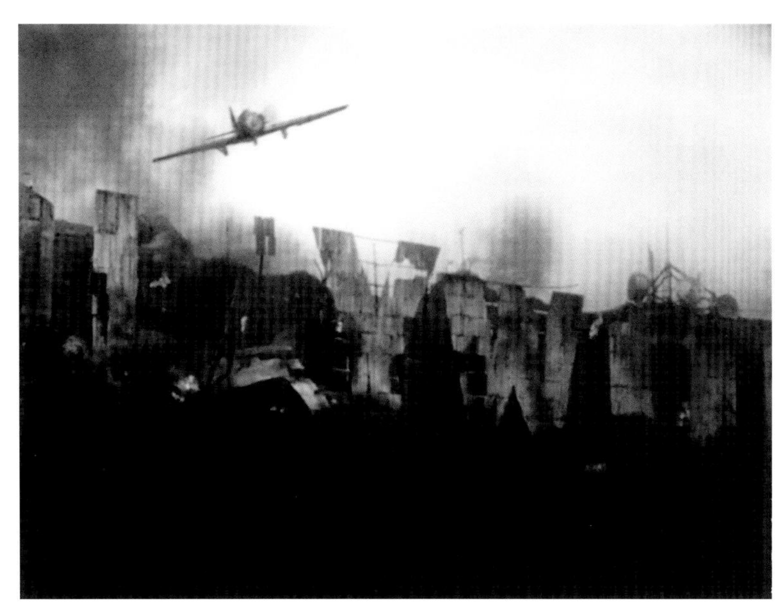

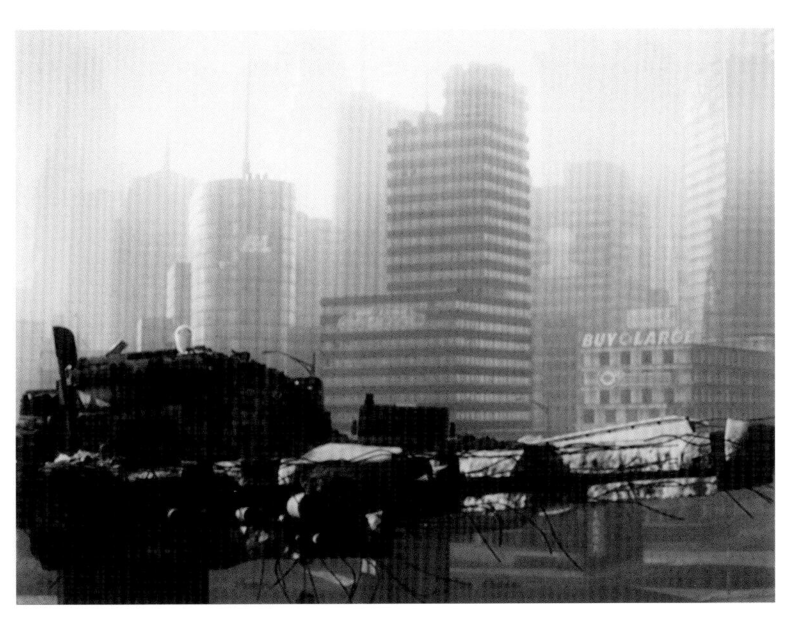

BUY N LARGE

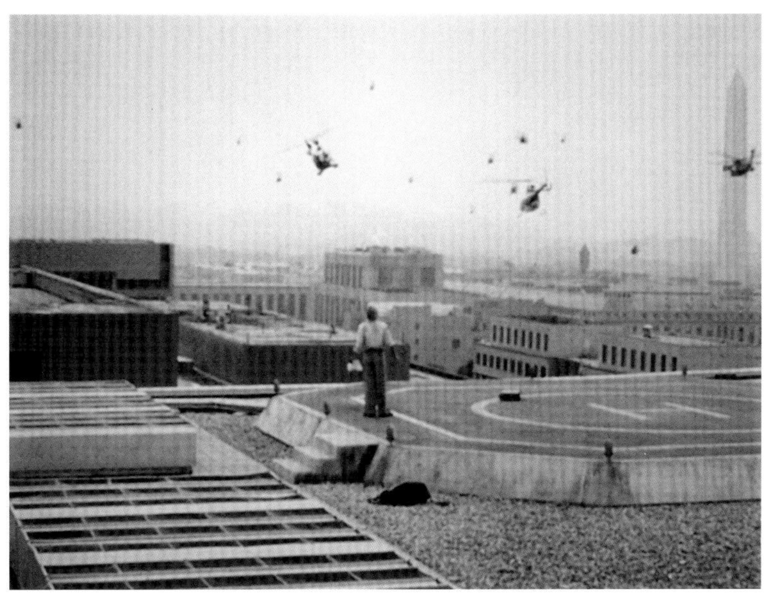

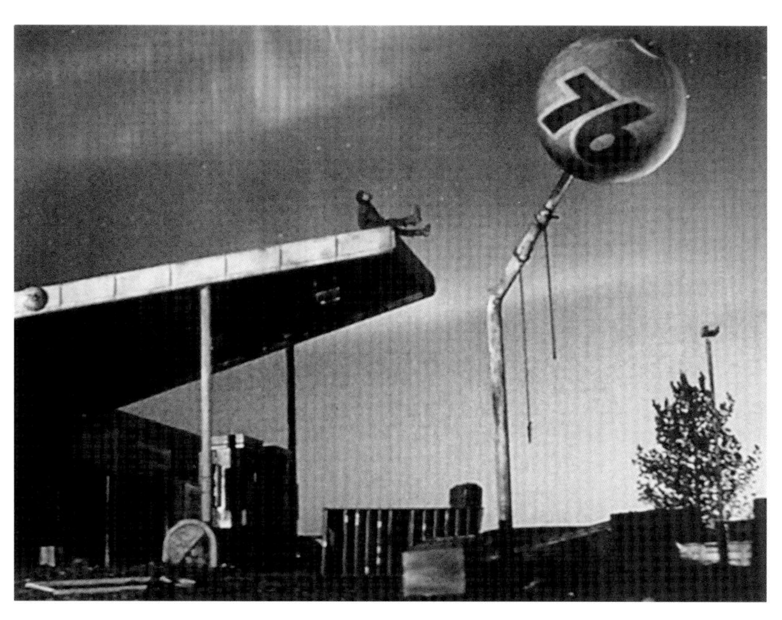

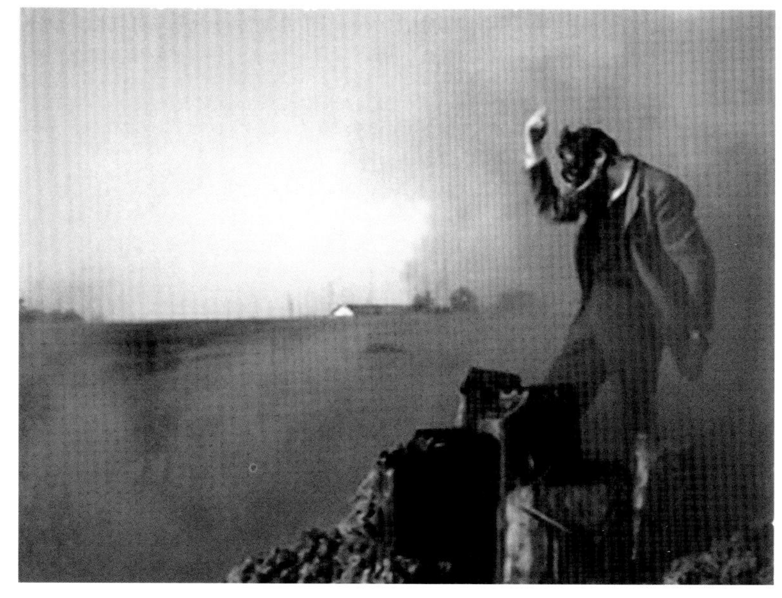

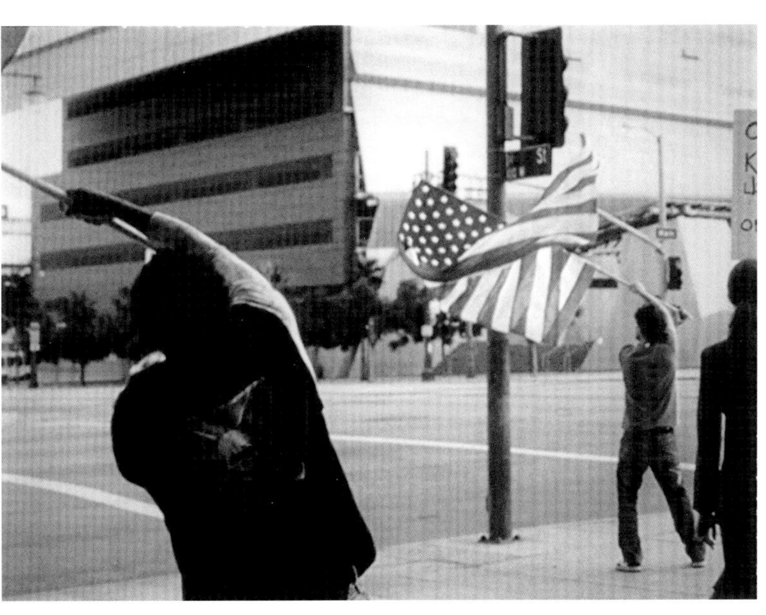
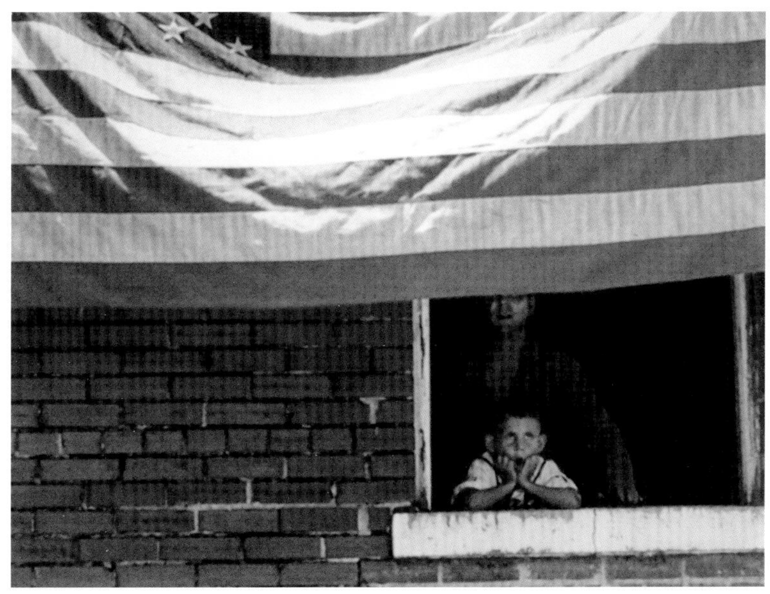

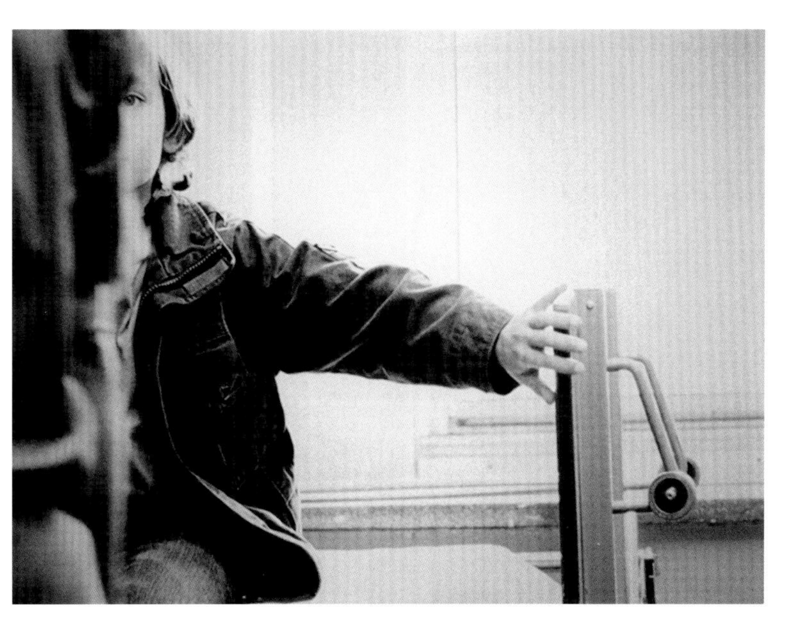

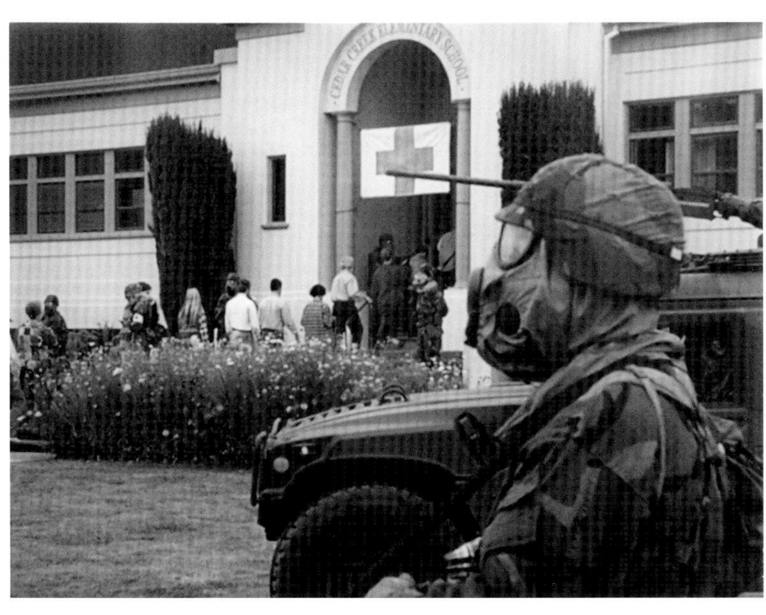

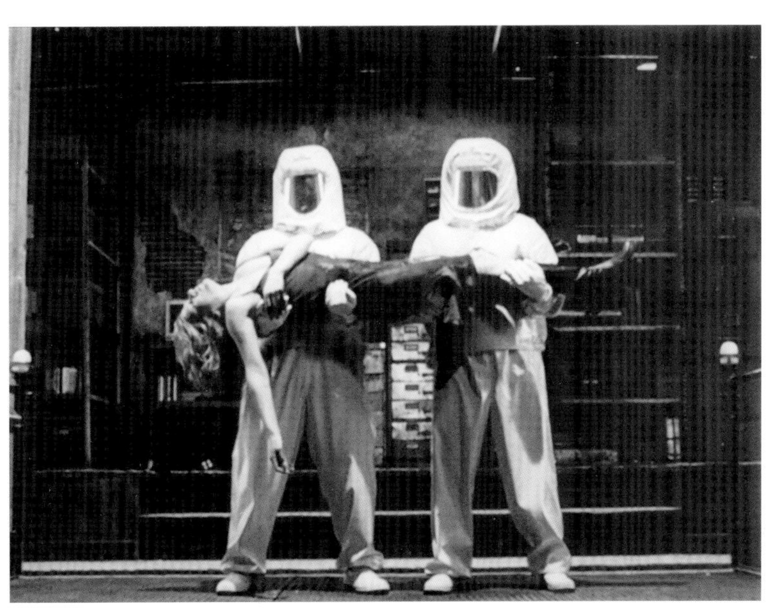

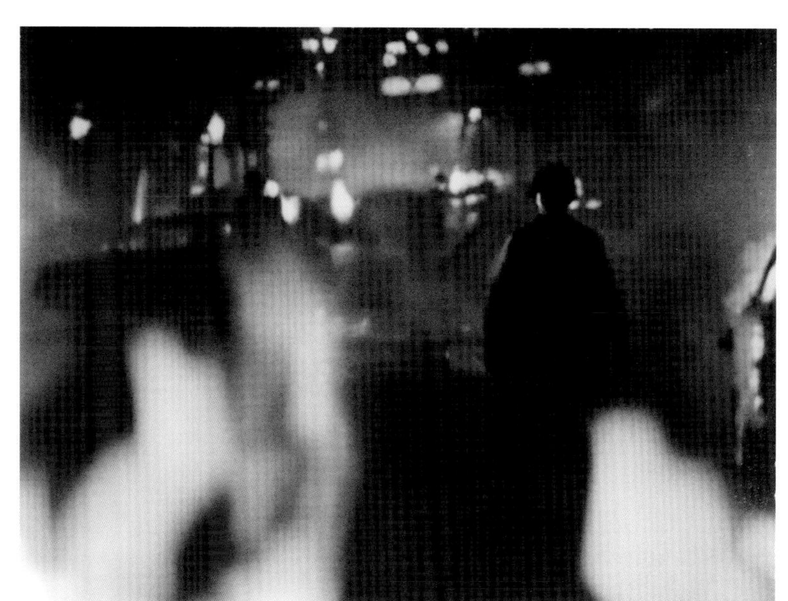

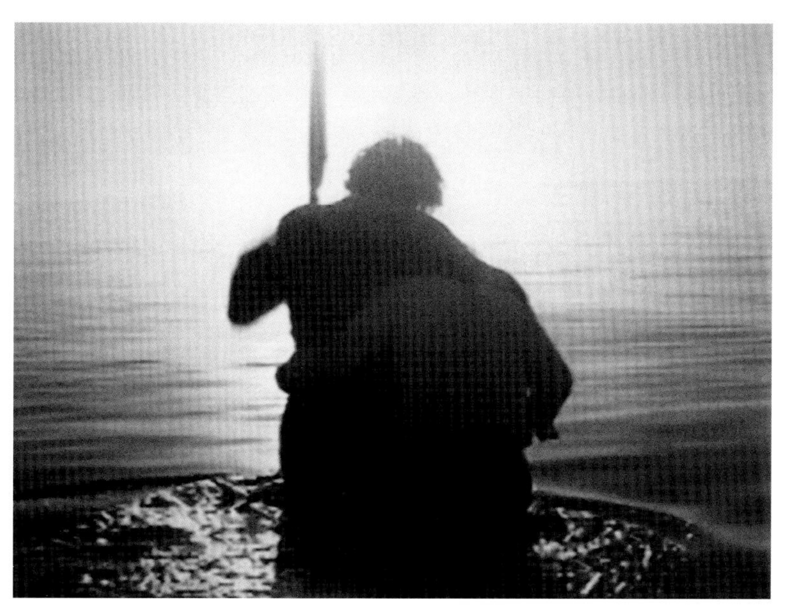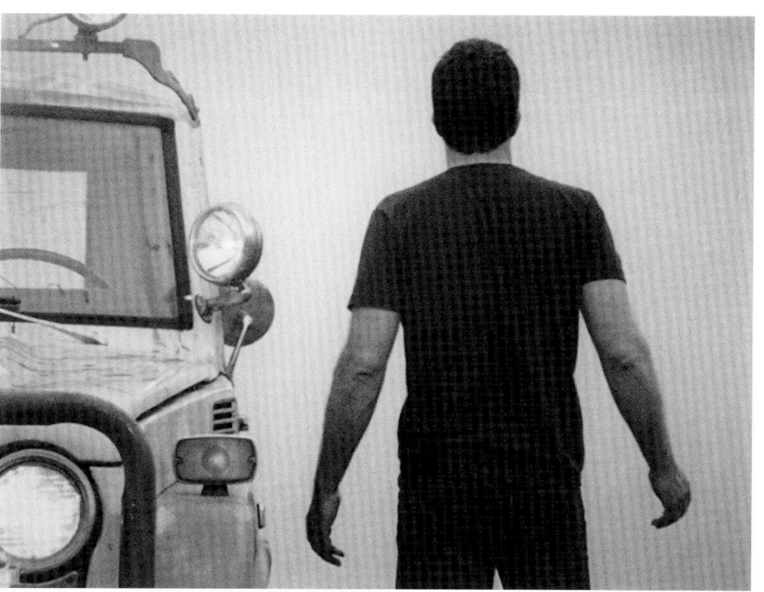

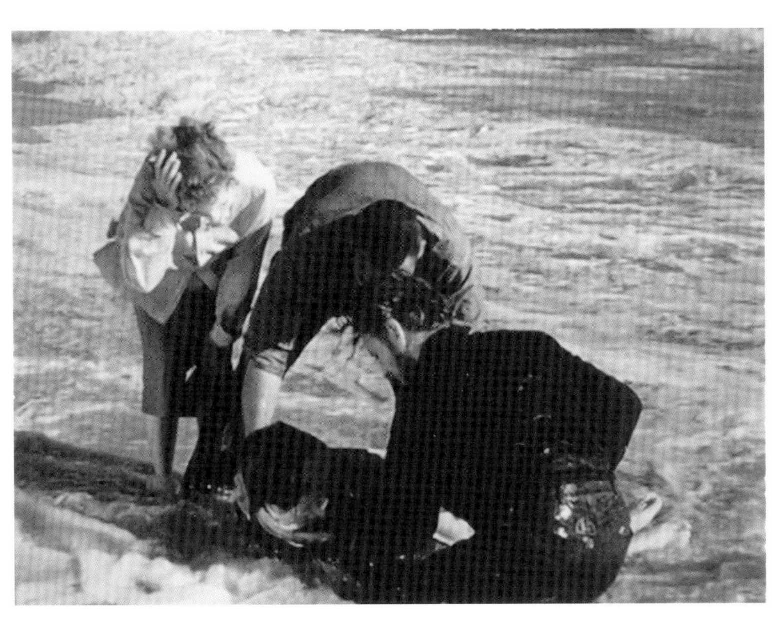 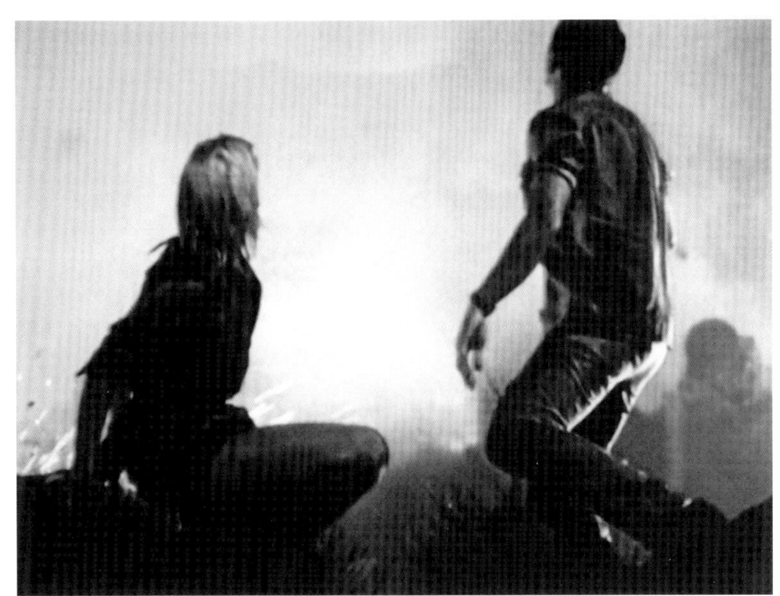

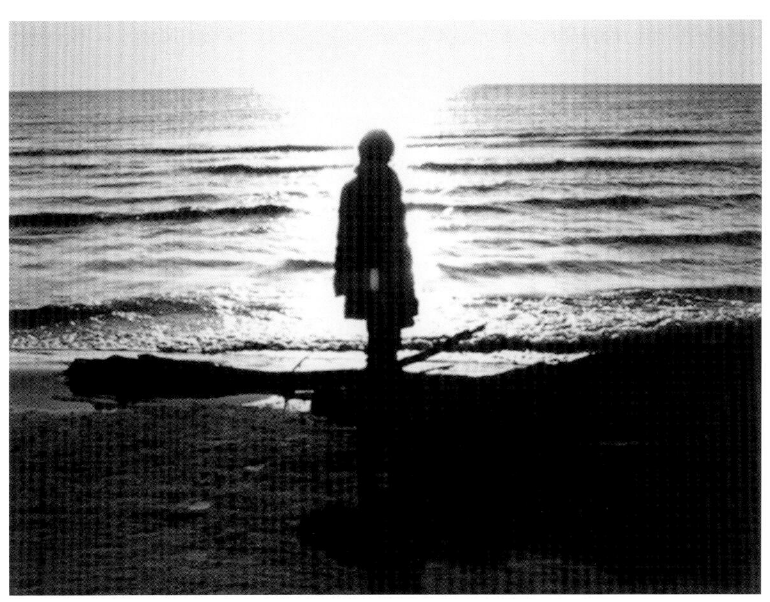

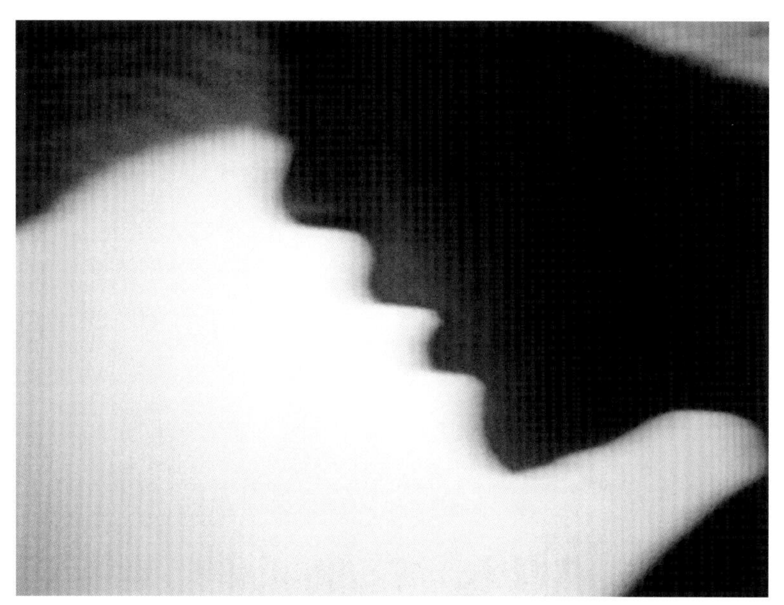

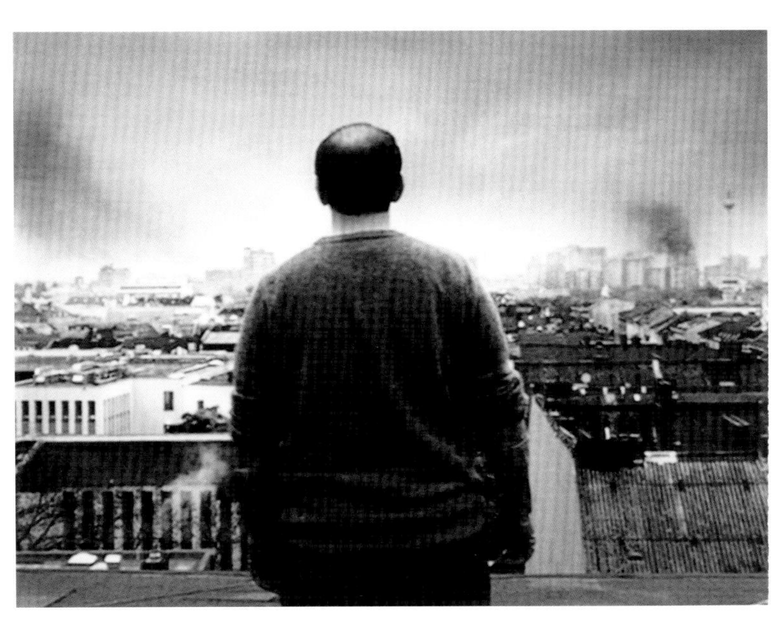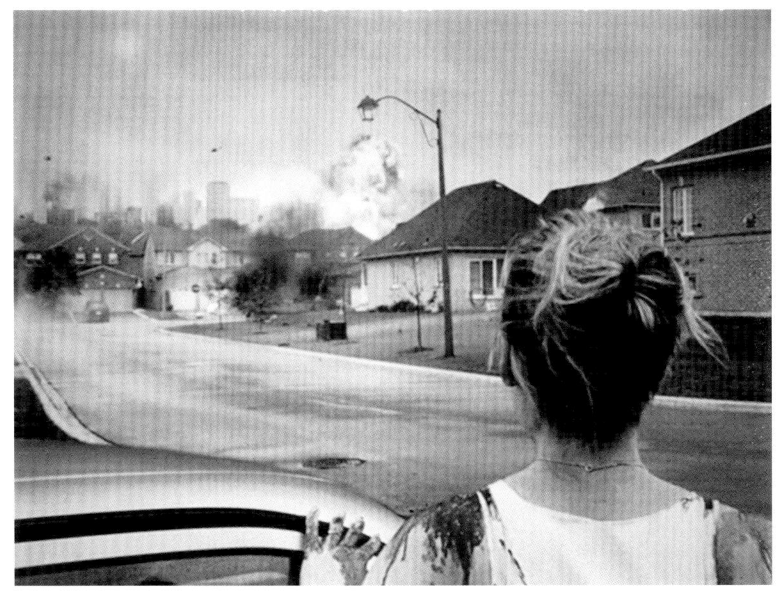

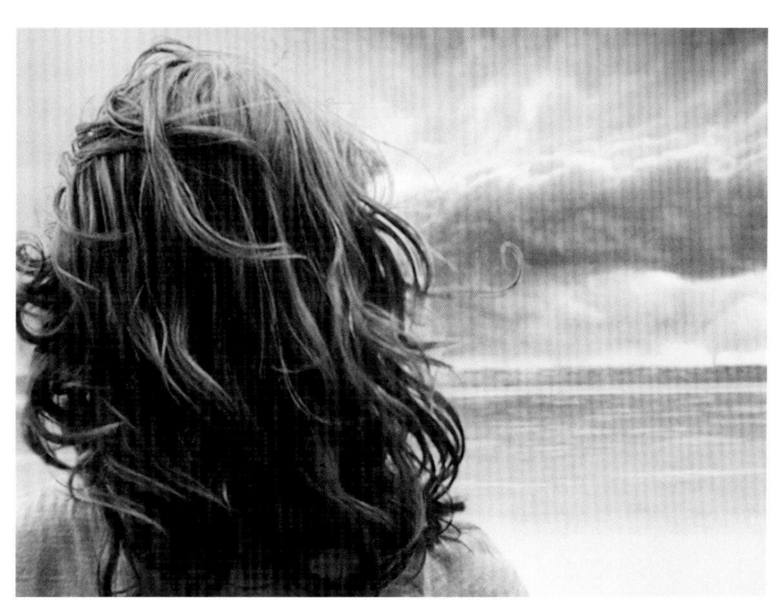

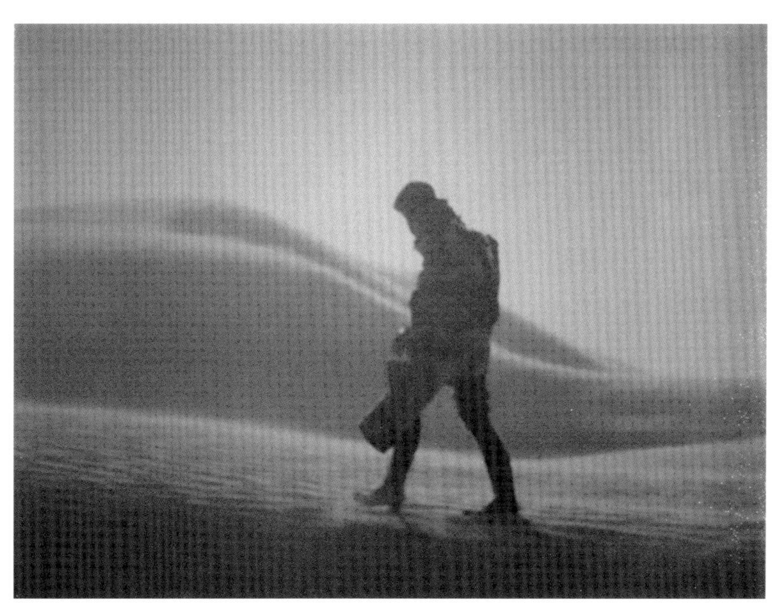

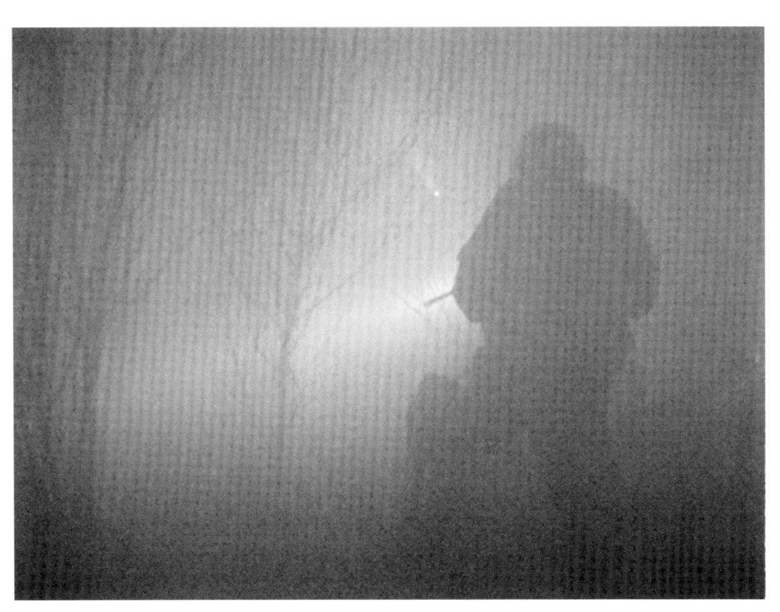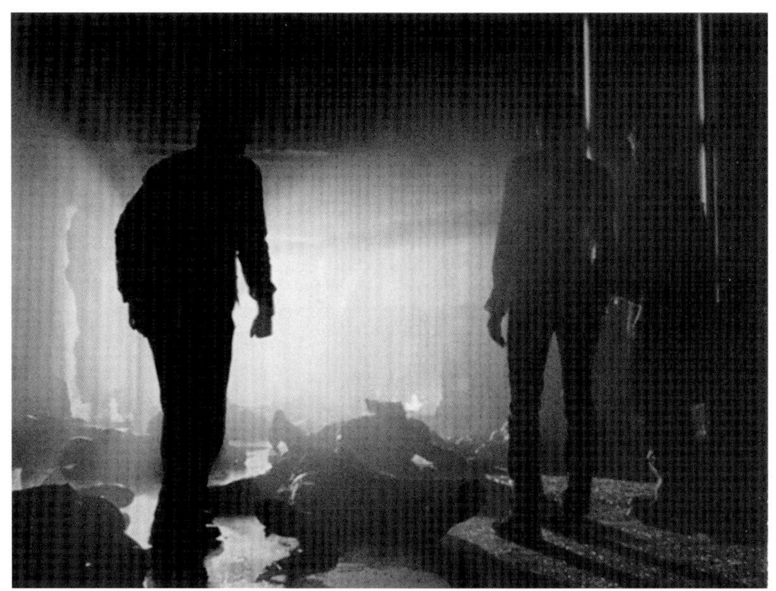

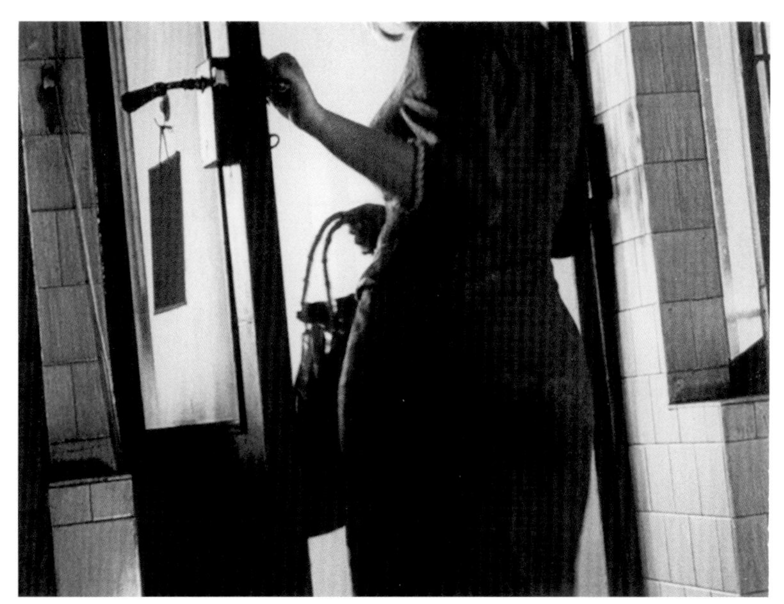

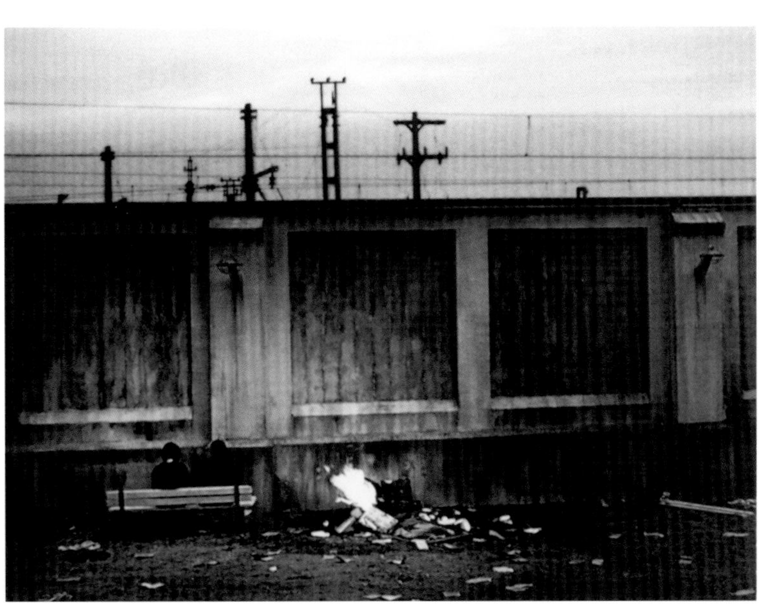

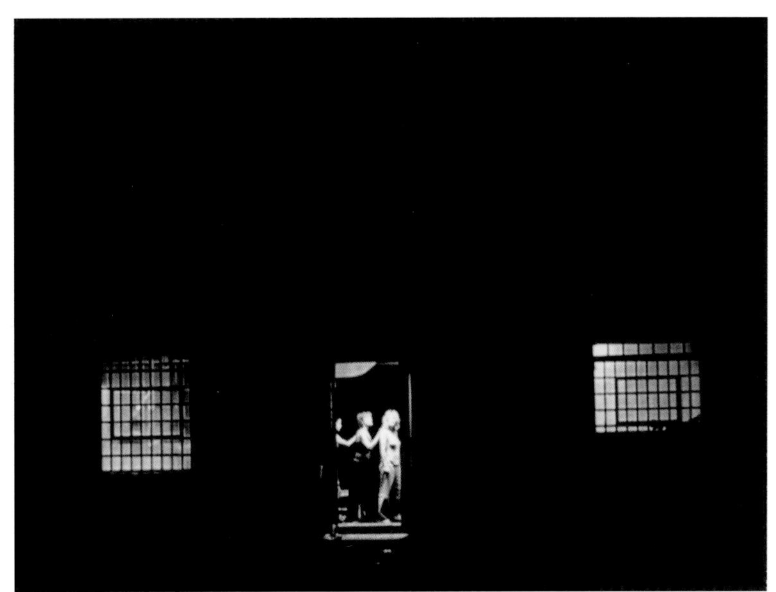

I would like to extend my gratitude to:

Leslie Jamison for contributing a sensitive, surprising essay that was the perfect thing I had no idea I was looking for. Your generosity and artistry are astounding.

Takaaki Okada for lending his unparalleled intellect and design acumen to this project. With finesse and aplomb you have elevated this project immeasurably.

Daniel Power for his steadfast support of this book and stalwartness as an independent book publisher. I am forevermore grateful to you for sharing my photographs with the world.

Craig Cohen for his patience and guidance with my first book and to the entire powerHouse team, present and future, for their continued support.

My parents and my sister for their unequivocal love, inspiration, and support. To say anything further would be an understatement.

Lena Valencia for facilitating this project, being constantly by my side, and having a heart and mind that are always open. Your love sustains me.

Mitch Epstein and Susan Bell for their early input and encouragement over the duration of this project. You are pillars of virtuosity and style I trust implicitly.

Lee Satkowski for lending his incisive eyes and ears as this thing took form. Thank you for connecting me and connecting with me.

Francesca Romeo for your boundless insight and decisive language which helped me define this project. I dearly hold your friendship and honesty.

Allen Frame for his ongoing audience and critique. I am not alone in considering you a bona fide treasure of the New York photography community.

Philip Perkis, and in memory of Dick Robinson and Louis Cicotello, whose tutelage I will always cherish.

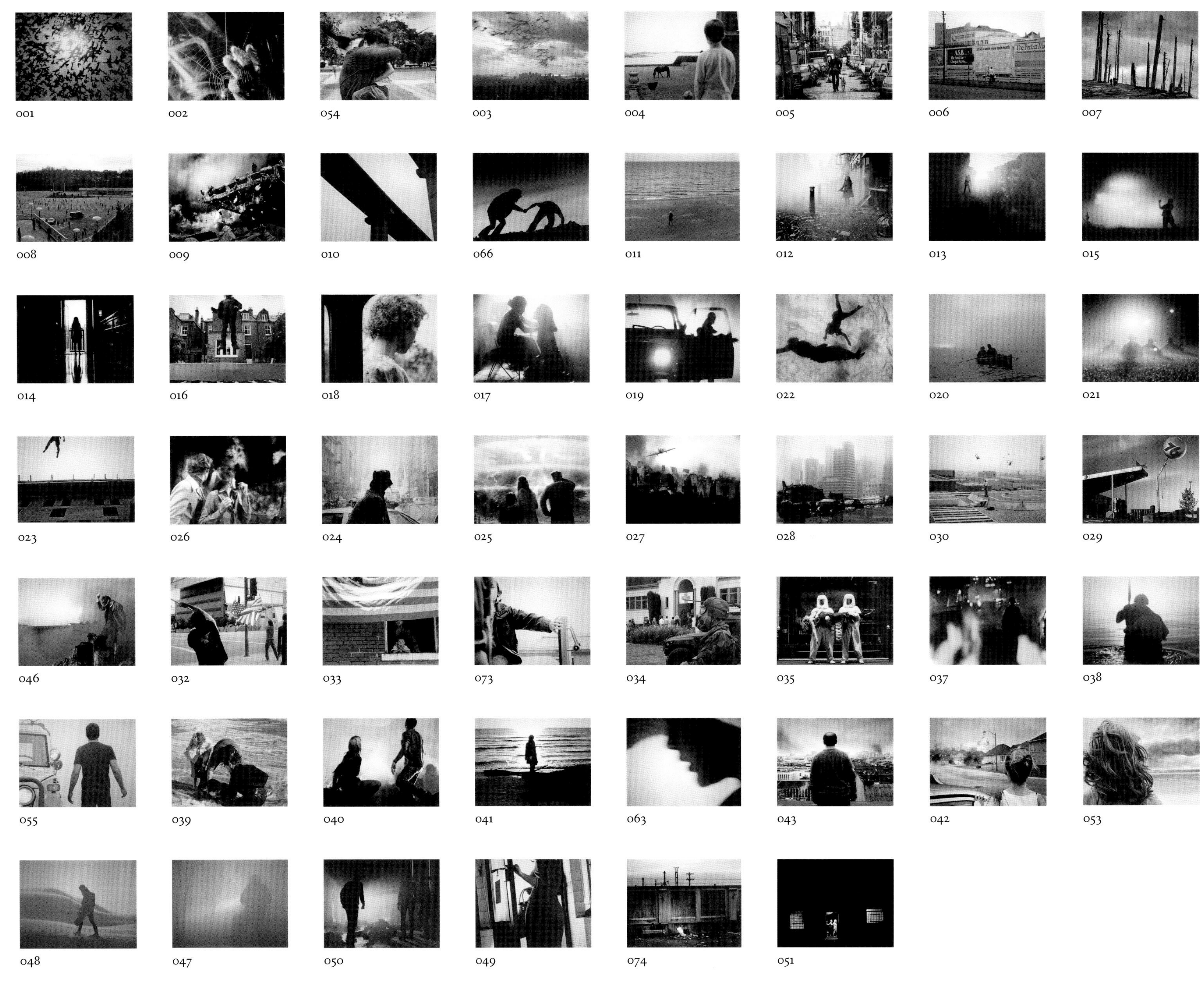